Go Out and Play!

FAVORITE OUTDOOR GAMES FROM

KaBOOM!®

CANDLEWICK PRESS

Thank you to Playworks for providing material for this book. Playworks is a national nonprofit organization that supports learning by providing safe, healthy, and inclusive play and physical activity to schools at recess and throughout the entire school day. Access even more free game recipes courtesy of Playworks at www.playworks.org/games.

First edition 2012

Library of Congress Cataloging-in-Publication Data is available.
Library of Congress Catalog Card Number pending

ISBN 978-0-7636-5530-3

11 12 13 14 15 16 TLF 10 9 8 7 6 5 4 3 2 1

Printed in Dongguan, Guangdong, China

This book was typeset in American Typewriter and Myriad Pro.
The illustrations were created digitally.

Candlewick Press
99 Dover Street
Somerville, Massachusetts 02144

visit us at www.candlewick.com

Contents

KaBOOM!

Dear Friends,

As an adult who has devoted my life to the cause of play, I want to thank you for being interested in getting outside and having fun the old-fashioned way — by playing. I believe all children everywhere should, when they grow up, have the same joy-filled memories I have of running, kicking, and dodging under a bright summer sun (and under gray skies on a cold winter day). All that anyone needs is some rules (which you can feel free to change), a bit of grass or asphalt, a ball, a rope, a can, some chalk, or just a determination to let loose and have fun.

If you are a parent, grandparent, or any adult who cares about children, let me be serious for just a bit. Sadly, play is disappearing from the lives of far too many children. Researchers point to many reasons for this. Too few places to play. Too much time spent watching television, playing video games, and online. Lack of recess in our schools. Unsafe neighborhoods. All these are indeed reasons children are playing less and less and spending way too little time outdoors. The nonprofit I founded is called KaBOOM!, and we are working hard to address these issues, because children who play are fitter and more creative, learn how to play well with others, and do better in school. Most important, children who play are happier.

The solution to what we call the play deficit begins, like so many problems, at home. Turn off the television, gather up your children and their friends, and go outside — to your front yard, your neighborhood park or playground — and start playing. If your kids are used to playing video games, they may resist. Be persistent. As a role model, you should lead by example. Start things off by playing with your kids yourself. And leave your electronic devices behind!

Every child should play outside for at least sixty minutes every day. And this book makes it easy to get started! There are lots of games here to choose from. Try a bunch. Choose your favorites. Get your friends and family to join you. I'd love to hear which games you like best. You can let me know at kaboom.org/gooutandplay. And feel free to make up your own games. Let me know about those, too.

Enough talk. Play!

Darell Hammond
Founder and CEO, KaBOOM!

Let's Get Started!

HOW TO FACILITATE CHILDREN'S PLAY

IT IS HARD to argue the benefits that play affords children. When children play, they develop the critical cognitive, social-emotional, and physical skills that will guide and support them as they move toward adulthood. The wonder of children's play is that it engages kids in a world of knowledge without seeming as if it were an imposed lesson. When children are given the freedom, space, and time to play, their worlds expand. They are driven to explore, follow, and develop their own interests.

Chances are that if you are reading this book, you are someone who is looking to get kids outdoors and enjoying playful activities. Whether the kids are family members, students, campers, or perhaps even you, this book is a great resource to engage anyone in a bit of play.

Play by definition is something that is freely chosen, child-directed, and intrinsically motivated. Yet one of the most challenging elements for adults when considering how to support children's play is navigating the fine line between facilitating play for children and dictating what children should be doing while at play. To help you avoid those pitfalls, we have included a few tips on the following page for you to consider.

MAKE PLAY A PRIORITY

Take your children to a neighborhood park or playground. If you believe play is important, include it in your daily routine.

BE INCLUSIVE

Help the group to determine how all children can be included in the activity. "Mary has a broken foot. How can we include her in the race?"

DESIGNATE A QUIET SPACE

Not every child wants to engage in every activity. Children (much like adults) may need a quite place to retreat to, away from high-activity areas.

BREAK THE RULES

Children seem to understand from day one that the rules of games ebb and flow with current interests. There is no mandate to follow the rules of a game to the letter.

ROLE-PLAY

Be willing to take on roles assigned by children. Children will often invite you into their play session if you are patient. You may be tossing around a Frisbee or becoming a dinosaur before long.

LET GO OF ADULT AGENDAS

Play represents an opportunity for children to explore and navigate the world on their own. Step back and allow children to choose what and how they would like to engage in an activity.

STEP IN WHEN NEEDED

We want kids to have opportunities to take risks and negotiate conflicts, but there are times when the situation begins to go beyond what is considered safe. Adults should be prepared to step in and ensure that the space is safe for all children.

PROVIDE LOOSE PARTS

Play can be extended and enriched by providing children with open-ended materials or items with no clear purpose (such as a cardboard box). A rich variety of materials allows children to be creative and make the most of their imaginations.

 AND FINALLY, HAVE FUN!

Tag Games

Flashlight Tag

How to Play:

Flashlight tag is a nighttime mix of tag and hide-and-seek. Play it in the summer, after the sun has gone down. Choose one player to be "It," and designate a jail area.

Give the flashlight to "It," who then counts to fifty while the rest of the players go hide. "It" then turns on the flashlight and sets out to find the other players. When someone is found, "It" flashes him or her with the flashlight and calls out his or her name. Caught players then have to wait in the jail.

The last player to be found is "It" in the next round.

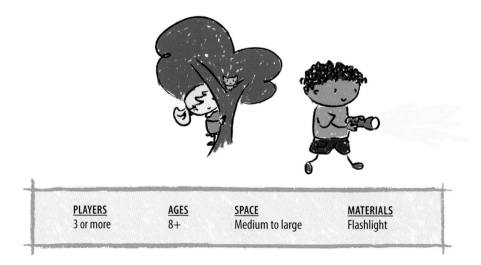

PLAYERS	AGES	SPACE	MATERIALS
3 or more	8+	Medium to large	Flashlight

Seaweed Tag

How to Play:

Mark off a large area to serve as the "ocean." One player, the "seaweed," stands in the middle of the ocean, while the rest of the players (the "fish") line up on the ends of the ocean. At "Ready, set, go!" the fish try to make it to the other side of the ocean without getting tagged by the seaweed.

If a fish is tagged by the seaweed, he or she also becomes seaweed but must keep one foot planted on the ground at all times while still trying to tag the other fish.

The fish who made it to the other side try to cross again, trying not to get tagged by the original or new seaweed. If they do, they also become seaweed. The last fish tagged is the first to act as seaweed for the next round.

PLAYERS	AGES	SPACE	MATERIALS
10 or more	5+	Medium to large	None

Partner Tag

How to Play:

Choose one player to be "It" and another player to be the runner. The rest of the players pair up and link arms. (If there are an odd number of players, then one group can be a group of three.)

The game starts when "It" tries to tag the runner before he or she has a chance to link up with another pair of players. Once the runner links arms with one of a pair, the player on the other side of the pair becomes the new runner. If "It" tags the runner, they switch roles and the runner becomes "It."

PLAYERS	AGES	SPACE	MATERIALS
8 or more	8+	Medium to large	None

Blob

How to Play:

Blob is a version of tag that just keeps growing. First choose one player to be the blob. The rest of the players then scatter and try not to get caught by the blob.

When the blob tags another player, they join hands and continue chasing the other players together. Each player that gets tagged joins the blob, which gets bigger and bigger.

When the last player is finally caught by the blob, that player starts the blob in the next round.

PLAYERS	AGES	SPACE	MATERIALS
4 or more	8+	Large	None

Sharks and Minnows

How to Play:

This is a game similar to tag in which "minnows" try to avoid the "sharks." Choose a large, open play area and set up two end zones between which players will run.

One player is chosen as the shark and stands at one end zone. The rest of the players stand together at the other end zone. They are the minnows.

When the shark calls out, "Come, little fishies!" the minnows try to run to the other end zone without getting tagged by the shark. Minnows who *do* get tagged become sharks.

The minnows continue to run back and forth until they have all become sharks.

The last minnow to be tagged then becomes the shark in the next round.

PLAYERS	AGES	SPACE	MATERIALS
5 or more	5+	Large	Cones or other objects to mark end zones

Shadow Tag

How to Play:

This version of tag needs to be played on a bright sunny day, on a playground or field where you can see your shadow.

Choose one player to be "It." He or she tries to tag the other players by stepping on their shadows on the ground.

When a player's shadow is tagged, he or she becomes "It."

PLAYERS	AGES	SPACE	MATERIALS
4 or more	All	Medium	None

Blindman's Bluff

How to Play:

Blindman's bluff is a traditional game that has been played by kids around the world for centuries. Be sure to play this game on a flat, grassy surface that is free of obstacles.

Choose one player to be the blind man. Place the blindfold over his or her eyes and lead him or her to the center of the play area. Next, the other players scatter while the blind man turns around five times, then calls out "Stop!"—at which point all the other players must stand in place. The blind man then moves around the play area, trying to grab one of the other players, who can move their bodies, but not their feet, to avoid the blind man's grasp. The other players can also make noises to confuse the blind man.

The first player tagged by the blind man becomes the blind man in the next round. Or you can play a different version of the game in which the blind man feels the tagged player's face to try to guess who it is. If the blind man guesses correctly, the tagged player becomes the blind man in the next round.

PLAYERS	AGES	SPACE	MATERIALS
8 or more	5+	Medium to large	Blindfold

Marco Polo

How to Play:

Marco Polo is similar to blindman's bluff and is often played in a swimming pool. But you can just as easily play it in an open yard or field (without any obstacles on the ground that are easy to trip over!).

One player is chosen to be "It." He or she then closes his or her eyes and calls out, "Marco!" The rest of the players then answer back, "Polo!" "It" tries to follow the sound of their voices in order to tag one of the other players.

When a player is tagged, that person is "It" in the next round.

Adapted from the Playworks Playbook

PLAYERS	AGES	SPACE	MATERIALS
4 or more	8+	Large field or swimming pool	None

Dog Chases Its Tail

How to Play:

All the players line up, and the last player in line takes the bandanna and places it in his or her back pocket so it hangs down like a dog's tail. All the players then place their hands on the hips of the players in front of them.

The front of the line then chases the back of the line, trying to grab the bandanna tail. The players in the middle can help or hinder the head or the tail, depending on their whims. If the line breaks, the player who let go must step out of the line, making it even shorter.

If you have enough players, you can set up two lines, creating two dogs that can chase each other's tails!

Adapted from the *Playworks Playbook*

PLAYERS	AGES	SPACE	MATERIALS
6 or more	8+	Large	Bandanna or handkerchief

Don't Get Caught with the Cookie

How to Play:

Choose two players to be taggers, then divide the rest into two equal groups. All the players in one group then take a ball or beanbag. The two taggers run after the other players, trying to tag the ones holding the balls or beanbags (called "cookies").

In order to avoid getting tagged, a player can pass his or her cookie to a player who is not already holding one. If a player with a cookie is tagged, the cookie goes in the cookie jar — a bucket or bag in the middle of the play area — and that player is out.

Play continues until all the players holding cookies are caught. For variety, you can limit the way the cookies get passed to other players, such as only from boy to girl or girl to boy, by rolling them on the ground, or by bouncing them once, and so on.

Adapted from the *Playworks Playbook*

PLAYERS	AGES	SPACE	MATERIALS
6 or more	5+	Large	Enough balls or beanbags for half of the players; a bucket or bag

Pickpocket Tag

How to Play:

Here is a fun twist on traditional tag that will have players picking their friends' pockets.

Each player places a strip of cloth in his or her pocket or waist-band. Players then run around the play area trying to grab the strips of cloth from other players' pockets. At the same time, they need to try to keep others from grabbing their own strip of cloth.

After everyone's pocket has been picked, the player who grabbed the most pieces of cloth wins.

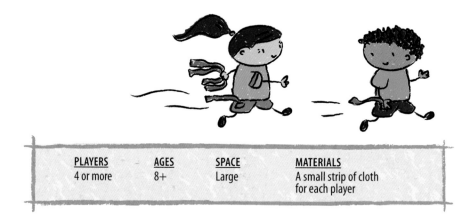

PLAYERS	AGES	SPACE	MATERIALS
4 or more	8+	Large	A small strip of cloth for each player

Fakeout

How to Play:

Draw two baselines about 20 feet apart (or mark them off some other way). Mark off the side boundaries by drawing two lines between the edges of the baselines, making a rectangle. Divide the players into two teams and have them line up behind each of the baselines. One team will be the "fakers," and the other team will be the "taggers."

On "Go!" the first two players from each team start moving toward the opposite baseline. The object is for the faker to try to run past the tagger and reach the other baseline without getting tagged. The faker can go in any direction but has to stay within the boundries. The tagger needs to tag the faker with both hands.

Once the faker is tagged or reaches the opposite baseline, he or she joins the taggers at the end of the line. The tagger then joins the end of the fakers' line. For variety and if you have a large enough group, try sending out two or three players from each team at once. Each tagger can then tag more than one faker.

Adapted from the *Playworks Playbook*

PLAYERS	AGES	SPACE	MATERIALS
6 or more	8+	Large	Chalk or some other way to indicate baselines

Hide-and-Seek Games

Hide-and-Seek

How to Play:

Choose a specific area (one with lots of hiding spots), and let players know what the boundaries are. Choose an object — perhaps a tree or rock — that will be considered home base. Choose one player to be the seeker. The rest of the players will hide that round. The seeker closes his or her eyes and counts to a predetermined number (it could be any number depending on the age of the players and the size of the area). While the seeker is counting, the rest of the players choose hiding spots. When he or she is done counting, the seeker calls out, "Ready or not, here I come!"

The seeker searches for the hiders. When a hider is found, the hider tries to run back to home base before the seeker tags him or her. Hiders who make it to home base are "safe." But if a hider is tagged before reaching home base, he or she becomes "It" in the next round.

PLAYERS	AGES	SPACE	MATERIALS
4 or more	5+	Large	None

Kick the Can

How to Play:

Kick the Can is closely related to hide-and-seek; the twist is that you don't actually have to tag people to catch them. First designate a jail area, and place the can there. Then choose someone to be "It." Someone else then kicks the can, and the players all scatter and hide. The player who is "It" retrieves the can, puts it back down in the jail area, and counts to fifty out loud.

"It" then goes out to find the players. If "It" sees someone, he or she goes back to the jail, picks up the can, taps three times, and calls out the person's name and hiding place—"I see Joey behind the blue car," for example. If "It" gets the name and hiding place right, the person hiding must come out and stay in the jail area.

Caught players may be freed from the jail if one of the other players not yet caught rushes to the jail and kicks the can before "It" can return to the jail and call out the can-kicker's name. If the can is kicked, "It" must run and pick it up, count to fifty, and go out searching for the other players again. Once "It" finds all the players, the first person caught is "It" in the next round.

PLAYERS	AGES	SPACE	MATERIALS
4 to 12	8+	Large grassy field or safe street	A clean, empty can

Sardines

How to Play:

Sardines is a lot like hide-and-seek, but backwards! Choose one player to be the first sardine. The rest of the players are the seekers; they close their eyes and count to fifty while the sardine runs and hides.

When the seekers are done counting, they split up and try to find the hiding sardine. As each seeker finds the sardine, he or she quietly joins the sardine in the hiding spot. As more and more players crowd into the hiding spot, they get packed in . . . like sardines!

When the players are all packed into a small space, it can be tough not to giggle and give away the hiding spot. The last seeker to find the hiding spot is the first sardine in the next round.

PLAYERS	AGES	SPACE	MATERIALS
3 or more	5+	Large	None

Ghosts in the Graveyard

How to Play:

Ghosts in the Graveyard is a spooky twist on hide-and-seek. It's best played in a yard or a park with plenty of hiding places. Choose a tree, lamppost, or porch to be the home base and choose one player to be the ghost. The ghost goes off to hide while the rest of the players stay at home base, counting off, "One o'clock, two o'clock, three o'clock . . ." all the way to "midnight!" They then yell, "Star light, star bright, I hope I see a ghost tonight!" and set off to find the ghost.

When a seeker or two gets near, the ghost jumps out to scare them. Those seekers call out, "Ghosts in the graveyard!" and *all* the seekers rush back to home base. On the way, the ghost tries to tag as many players as he or she can.

Those who make it to home base are safe, but the tagged players become ghosts and join the first ghost as hiders in the next round. Play continues until all the players are ghosts.

PLAYERS	AGES	SPACE	MATERIALS
4 or more	8+	Large	None

Ball Games

Catch This!

How to Play:

The two players stand about ten steps away from each other, one of them holding all the balls.

The player with the balls throws one to the other player so that he or she can catch it. After the ball is caught, the catcher holds on to it, and then the thrower throws another ball, and then another and another, seeing how many the catcher can still catch while holding on to to all the other balls.

When the catcher finally drops one of the balls, the players switch roles. The person who can catch the most balls wins!

PLAYERS	AGES	SPACE	MATERIALS
2	5+	Small to medium	Small soft foam balls or socks rolled up into balls

Down, Down, Down

How to Play:

Down, Down, Down is a variation on the game of catch, with penalties for dropping the ball.

Two players stand facing each other about eight to ten steps apart and start tossing the ball back and forth, trying not to drop it. The players continue, each trying to catch the ball cleanly without dropping it, until one of them drops the ball.

When a player drops the ball, he or she needs to go down to the ground on one knee and then continue catching and throwing from that position.

If the player drops the ball again, he or she must then kneel down on both knees. Each time the ball is dropped, the player has to get lower and lower, adding one elbow, then two elbows, and finally his or her chin! If play proceeds for a while without anyone dropping the ball, have the players take a step back each time they make a clean catch to make it more of a challenge.

On a hot day, try playing with a water balloon!

PLAYERS	AGES	SPACE	MATERIALS
2	5+	Medium	A tennis ball

Running Bases

How to Play:

Set up two bases about 30 feet apart. Depending on the number of players, your bases could be real bases, cones, or two circles drawn on the ground with chalk.

Select two players to be the throwers. They will guard the bases. The other players are the runners. To start the game, the runners stand in the middle, between the two bases. Once the first throw is thrown, the runners all run to one of the bases. The throwers then toss the ball back and forth while the runners run from one base to the other.

While a runner is on base, he or she is safe. But if a runner is between bases, he or she can get tagged with the ball by one of the throwers. (The ball is held in the hand, not thrown at the runner!) If a runner is tagged, he or she gets one "out." If a runner gets three outs, he or she is out of the game. The last runner standing wins. The last two runners are the throwers for the next game.

PLAYERS	AGES	SPACE	MATERIALS
4 to 12	8+	Large	A tennis ball; 2 bases

Wall Ball

How to Play:

To play wall ball, you'll need a wall without any windows and with a good amount of open space in front of it. With chalk or tape, first mark a short line on the ground about 15 feet from the wall.

The first player has the ball and is the thrower, while the other player is the fielder. The thrower stands behind the short line and throws the ball toward the wall, making it bounce once on the ground before it hits the wall. The fielder attempts to catch the ball in the air after it leaves the wall. If the fielder makes a successful catch, he or she becomes the thrower.

If the fielder doesn't catch the ball, the thrower gets a point and continues throwing. All throws must hit the ground before hitting the wall and must also clear the short line on the way back. If a throw does not hit the ground first or clear the short line, a foul is called.

A thrower's turn is over after two fouls occur during the same turn (not necessarily in a row). The first player to reach 10 points wins.

PLAYERS	AGES	SPACE	MATERIALS
2	8+	Large space with a wall	A tennis or rubber ball; a wall; chalk or tape

Name-It Ball

How to Play:

Players stand in a circle. One player chooses a category such as "Ice-Cream Flavors."

The starting player names something in that category, "Vanilla," for example, then bounces the ball to another person in the circle.

The next player must say another word in the same category, such as "Chocolate chip." He or she then bounces the ball to another player.

When a player cannot name something new in the category, he or she is out.

The last player standing gets to choose the category for the next round.

PLAYERS	AGES	SPACE	MATERIALS
3 or more	5+	Medium	A basketball or other ball that bounces

Five Hundred

How to Play:

One player is the thrower and the rest are catchers. The thrower throws the ball up in the air and says a number between one and five hundred (it's best to stick to round numbers like one hundred, two hundred, etc.).

Whoever catches the ball receives the number of points called out by the thrower.

Catchers keep track of how many points they've received. The first to reach 500 is the winner, and he or she becomes the thrower in the next round.

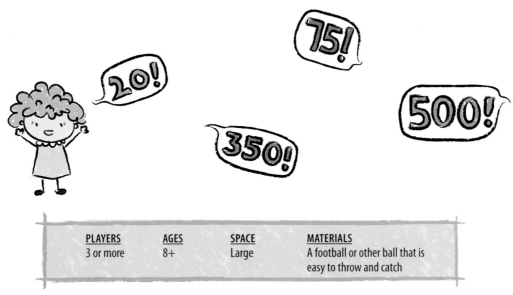

PLAYERS	AGES	SPACE	MATERIALS
3 or more	8+	Large	A football or other ball that is easy to throw and catch

Push Catch

How to Play:

Choose one player to be the thrower, and have the rest of the players form a big circle around him or her. The thrower then goes around the circle, tossing the ball to each player in turn. As the ball is thrown, the thrower calls out either "Catch!" or "Push!" If the thrower says "Catch," the player has to catch the ball, and if the thrower says "Push," the player has to push the ball back to the thrower.

If the player gets it right, he or she remains in the game. If not, then he or she is out. Play continues until there is one player left, who becomes the thrower in the next round.

The thrower should first go around the circle in order but can then go in random order around the circle, trying to catch the players off guard.

Adapted from the Playworks Playbook

PLAYERS	AGES	SPACE	MATERIALS
6 or more	5+	Medium	A beach ball, kickball, or other soft ball

Bubbles

How to Play:

The object of this game is very simple: keep the ball in the air as long as you can! Stand together in an open field or playground and throw the ball in the air.

Players keep hitting the ball to keep it in the air, but each player can hit the ball only one time in a row—a new player has to hit the ball each time. Players can use any part of their bodies to keep the ball in the air, too.

If you have a larger group of players, try adding another beach ball, and another!

Adapted from the *Playworks Playbook*

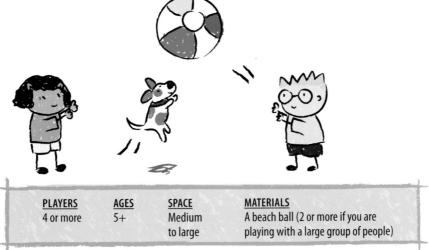

PLAYERS	AGES	SPACE	MATERIALS
4 or more	5+	Medium to large	A beach ball (2 or more if you are playing with a large group of people)

Around the World

How to Play:

Mark off five spots in a wide semicircle in front of the basket with either chalk or cones. You can number the spots one through five, starting with the marker closest to the basket on the right side and continuing around the semicircle.

The first player tries to make a basket from spot number one. If the ball goes in, he or she then moves to spot number two and tries to make the next shot. The same player keeps going around the semi-circle until a shot is missed.

Then the second player starts at spot number one and continues until a shot is missed. Once all the players have gone, the first player is up again and begins where he or she left off. The first player to make it "around the world," making a basket at all five spots, is the winner!

If you don't have a basketball court, you could also play this game with tennis balls and a bucket, or bean bags and a chalk-drawn circle. Use your imagination!

Adapted from the *Playworks Playbook*

PLAYERS	AGES	SPACE	MATERIALS
3 or more	8+	Medium	A basketball; basketball court; cones or chalk

Clean Your Room

How to Play:

Divide into two equal teams, with one person serving as the time-keeper. Place an equal number of balls on either side of the net.

First, the timekeeper decides how long the game will last. When the timekeeper says "Go!" each team tries to "clean their room" by throwing as many balls as they can over to the other side of the net during the specified time.

The other team then picks up the balls and throws as many as they can back! When time is up, the timekeeper calls out "Stop!" and the balls on each side are counted.

The team with the least number of balls on their side of the net wins.

Adapted from the *Playworks Playbook*

PLAYERS	AGES	SPACE	MATERIALS
8 or more	5+	Large	Volleyball net; lots of balls — could be volleyballs, kickballs, or tennis balls

Baby in the Air

How to Play:

Each player is assigned a number. If there are four people playing, for example, each player is given a number between one and four.

The starting player throws the ball up in the air while calling out, "Baby in the air, number . . ." followed by a number of one of the players. The player whose number is called runs to catch the ball. At the same time, the other players try to get as far away as possible.

When the player catches the ball, he or she yells "Freeze!" and the other players must stop where they are.

The player with the ball is then allowed to take three steps in any direction. He or she tries to tag one of the other players with the ball. If the player with the ball tags another player, the tagged player receives the letter *B*. If the player with the ball misses, he or she receives a *B*.

The player who caught the ball then throws it into the air and calls out another number to begin the next round.

As the game goes along, players receive the letters *B*, then *A*, then *B*, then *Y*. When a player spells *BABY*, he or she is out. The last player left is the winner.

PLAYERS	AGES	SPACE	MATERIALS
4 or more	8+	Large	A dodgeball or other soft ball

Coconut Bowling

How to Play:

Coconut bowling lets you set up a bowling alley right in your own park!

Start by filling the empty bottles with an inch or two of water. These are your pins. Set them up in a triangle, with one bottle in the first row, two in the second, and three in the third.

Mark a starting line about 10 to 20 feet away from the pins. Then stand behind the starting line and roll the coconut toward the bottles, just like in bowling.

You can keep score if you like, or just play for fun!

Submitted by a Play Day participant

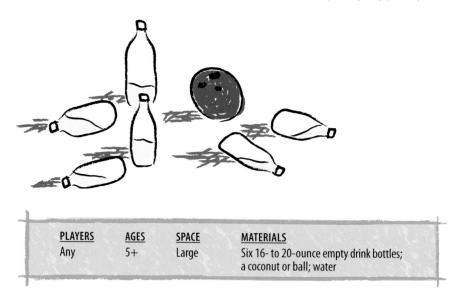

PLAYERS	AGES	SPACE	MATERIALS
Any	5+	Large	Six 16- to 20-ounce empty drink bottles; a coconut or ball; water

Ring of Fire

How to Play:

If you already have a disc golf basket in your park or yard, have everyone take a Frisbee and stand in a wide circle around it, about 20 to 40 feet away.

If you don't have a disc golf basket, you can use a large tub, like a kiddie pool, or even a pole or a tree.

On the count of three, have everyone throw his or her Frisbee at the same time, aiming for the goal. The player who makes the basket or hits the target wins that round.

If two or more players make the basket, those players try again until just one person succeeds. Play continues until someone wins five rounds.

Submitted by a Play Day participant

PLAYERS	AGES	SPACE	MATERIALS
5 or more	8+	Large	A Frisbee for each player; a disc golf basket or a large tub or bucket

Team Games

Scavenger Hunt

How to Play:

Create a list of ten natural objects that are likely to be found in your local park or around your neighborhood. Your list could include anything from a dandelion to a grasshopper, a rock, an oak tree, or a feather.

Make sure everybody writes down the same list of items to find. Depending on the number of people in your group, divide into small search teams. Once everybody is ready, start the hunt!

As you search for the items, you can simply cross them off your list, collect them (as long as your list doesn't include living things), or use a camera to take pictures of what you find.

You can set a time limit and see which team finds the most objects or see which team can finish the entire list first.

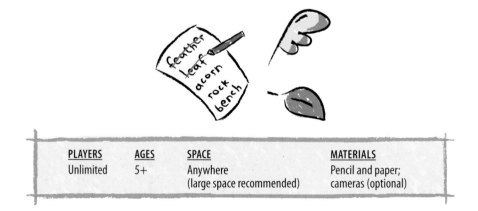

PLAYERS	AGES	SPACE	MATERIALS
Unlimited	5+	Anywhere (large space recommended)	Pencil and paper; cameras (optional)

Capture the Flag

How to Play:

Split up into two teams, and give each team an equal amount of territory on either side of the playing area (for example, front and back yards, opposite sides of the school, indoors versus outdoors). Give teams five minutes to hide their flag somewhere in their territory.

During this period, teams can send out spies to see where the opposing team's flag is being hidden, as well as lookouts to tag the opposing team's spies if they venture into "enemy" territory. If a spy is tagged, he or she must go to jail and can be freed only if tagged by a teammate. When the flag is hidden, call out that the team is finished.

The players then line up, and someone says "Go!" to start the game and begin to search for the other team's flag. As with spies, if a player is tagged by an opponent on the opposing team's territory, he or she must go to jail and can be freed only if tagged by a teammate.

The first team to capture the opposing team's flag and bring it back to their side wins!

PLAYERS	AGES	SPACE	MATERIALS
10 or more	8+	Large (grassy field with places to hide a plus)	2 flags; 8 cones to set up the jail; something to mark boundaries with

Big-Base Kickball

How to Play:

The rules are similar to those of baseball. Select a field or an open asphalt area. Lay out home plate, first, second, and third bases 60 feet (20 paces) apart. The pitching mound should be 42 feet (14 paces) from home plate.

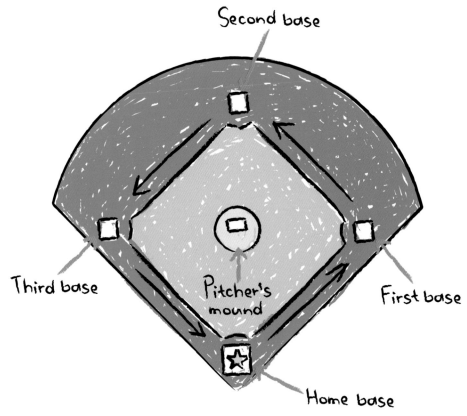

Second base

Third base

Pitcher's mound

First base

Home base

Divide your group into two teams. On the field, you'll have a pitcher, first, second, and third basemen, three outfielders, a shortstop, and a catcher. The kicking team determines the "kicking order" before the game starts, and it remains the same for the entire game. The pitcher must pitch underhand, with no spinning or throwing, and the ball must be rolled below the kicker's knees.

Kicking rules: four balls (bad or outside pitches) mean the kicker walks to first base; four fouls mean the kicker is automatically out. Instead of counting outs, let everyone on the team get a chance to kick.

In big-base kickball, you are allowed to have an unlimited number of players on a base at one time.

A runner is out if the base he or she is running to is tagged or if he or she is tagged with the ball below the neck.

After a preset number of innings are played (usually five or six), the team with the most runs wins.

PLAYERS	AGES	SPACE	MATERIALS
2 teams of 9 players	8+	Large open area or baseball diamond	A kickball; 4 bases

Red Rover

How to Play:

Split up into two teams of equal size. The teams line up on opposite sides of the play area and link hands. The first team starts by choosing someone on the other team (whom we'll call Jessica), calling out, "Red rover, red rover, let Jessica come over!"

Jessica lets go of her teammates' hands and sprints toward the other team, trying to break through their line. If she doesn't get through, she has to join that team.

If she does get through, she takes one player from that team, and they both go back and join Jessica's team.

The teams take turns calling over a member of the other team until one side has all the players.

PLAYERS	AGES	SPACE	MATERIALS
6 or more	8+	Medium-size grassy field	None

Crab Soccer

How to Play:

This game is played the same way as regular soccer, except that the players have to crawl along the ground like crabs!

Divide the group into two even teams. Then mark the field of play and set up two goals using cones. To get in the crab position, players sit down with both feet and hands on the ground. Once the game starts, the players lift their behinds and move around using their hands and feet, trying to score a goal. Remember, no hands are allowed in soccer, so players may move the ball only with their feet.

Each team is allowed to have one goalie, who also has to crawl like a crab but can use his or her hands to stop the ball.

The first team to score 5 points wins the game!

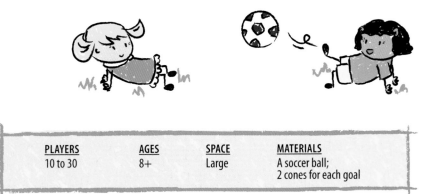

PLAYERS	AGES	SPACE	MATERIALS
10 to 30	8+	Large	A soccer ball; 2 cones for each goal

Pony Express

How to Play:

Pony Express is a fast mix of relay racing and tag. The object is to run a relay race while trying to catch up and tag the other team's runner.

Mark off a square or rectangular track and place a cone at opposite corners. Divide the players into two teams, and have them line up at each of the cones.

The first runner from each team takes a beanbag and, at the signal, they both start running in the same direction around the track. When they complete a lap, they pass the beanbag to the next runner. While running around the track, each runner tries to catch up to the other team's runner and tag him or her on the shoulder. If he or she succeeds, his or her team gets a point and a new round begins.

To change things up and have some fun, try doing something other than running, such as hopping, skipping, or speed walking.

Adapted from the *Playworks Playbook*

PLAYERS	AGES	SPACE	MATERIALS
4 or more	8+	Large	Two beanbags, batons, or small balls; chalk to mark off the track; two cones

Steal the Bacon

How to Play:

First name a referee, then divide the remaining players up into two equal teams. The players on both teams should count off so that each player shares a number with a player on the other team.

Take the chalk and draw two lines on opposite sides of the playing area and a circle in the center. Have the teams line up on opposite lines, and place the bacon in the circle. The referee starts the game by calling out a number.

The two players who have that number come out and try to take the bacon before their opponent, then run back past their team's line before getting tagged by the other player. If the player with the bacon makes it back to the line, that team gets a point. If he or she is tagged first, then no point is awarded.

The bacon is then returned to the circle, the referee calls out another number, and another pair of opponents tries to steal the bacon. The first team to reach 10 points wins.

PLAYERS	AGES	SPACE	MATERIALS
7 or more	8+	Large	Chalk; a small, easy-to-grab object to be the bacon, such as a stuffed toy, glove, or baton

Sidewalk Games

Hopscotch

How to Play:

Hopscotch has been played since ancient times — it started in Britain during the time of the Romans! You can find a painted hopscotch board on many playgrounds, but if there isn't one, you can easily draw one with chalk on a sidewalk, playground, or even a driveway.

The first player tosses his or her marker into the first square (marked "1"). The marker has to land completely within the square without touching a line or bouncing out. If the marker doesn't land in the right square, he or she forfeits his or her turn.

If the marker lands successfully, the player hops through the squares, avoiding the square containing the marker. Single squares must be hopped on with one foot, while side-by-side squares are landed on with both feet.

At the end of the board, the player turns around and comes back, pausing to pick up the marker. If he or she steps on a line or loses his or her balance while hopping through the squares, he or she is out and the next player takes a turn.

If the player is successful, he or she throws the marker into the next numbered square and goes again. The first player to complete all the squares on the court wins!

Adapted from *New York Street Games*

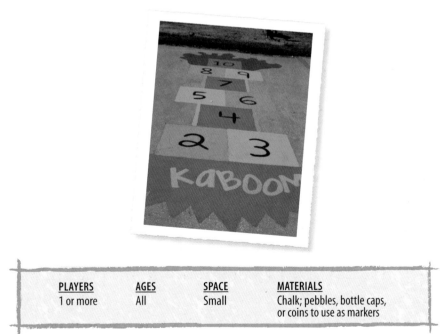

PLAYERS	AGES	SPACE	MATERIALS
1 or more	All	Small	Chalk; pebbles, bottle caps, or coins to use as markers

Four Square

How to Play:

Use chalk or tape to mark a 10 foot by 10 foot square on the ground, then divide it into four equal squares. Number the squares one to four, and have the first four players each stand in a square. The number-one square is the highest-ranking and is called the Ace. If there are more than four players, the other players should line up near the number-four (or lowest-ranking) square.

To start the game, the player acting as the Ace bounces the ball once in his or her own square and then hits it toward one of the other squares. The receiving player lets the ball bounce once in his or her square and then hits it to any other player. Play continues until one of the players makes a foul by hitting the ball before it bounces once in his or her square, by allowing the ball to bounce twice in his or her square, or by hitting the ball out of bounds.

When a player makes a foul, he or she moves down to the lowest-ranking square. Or, if there are more than four players, he or she moves to the end of the line. The other players then move up to fill the empty spots.

PLAYERS	AGES	SPACE	MATERIALS
4 or more	8+	Small concrete surface	A kickball; chalk or tape

Snail

How to Play:

Snail is a twisty variation of hopscotch. Start by drawing a large spiral on the ground using chalk. Then draw lines within the spiral, splitting it into segments. There can be as many segments as you like. That's the snail's shell. You can also draw the snail's head.

To start the game, each player stands on or near the snail's head and tosses a pebble onto one of the segments in the snail's shell. Then the players take turns hopping through the segments toward the center of the spiral, skipping over any segments that have pebbles in them, then turning around and hopping back through the segments to the snail's head.

If a player steps on a line or hops onto a segment that has a pebble, he or she is out. In the next round, try making it harder by hopping on one foot or by having to pick up all the pebbles on the way back and retossing pebbles for each player's turn.

PLAYERS	AGES	SPACE	MATERIALS
2 to 6	All	Medium concrete surface	Chalk; pebbles

Circle Games

Duck, Duck, Goose

How to Play:

Choose one player to be "It." The rest of the players sit in a circle facing each other. "It" walks or skips around the outside of the circle, gently tapping each player's head in turn, calling out "Duck!" with each tap.

Eventually "It" taps one of the players' heads and calls "Goose!" The player who was tapped gets up and chases "It" around the circle. "It" tries to make it back to the tapped player's empty seat before getting tagged.

If "It" does make it back, the goose becomes "It" for the next round. If "It" gets tagged, he or she has to sit in the middle of the circle. The goose then becomes "It" for the next round.

Meanwhile, the player in the middle can't leave until another player is tagged and takes his or her place.

PLAYERS	AGES	SPACE	MATERIALS
8 or more	All	Small	None

Hot Potato

How to Play:

Have you ever heard the phrase "dropped like a hot potato"? In this game, you don't drop the hot potato but try to pass it to another person as quickly as possible.

One player is the "caller" while the rest of the players stand in a circle and begin passing the ball or beanbag from one person to the next, pretending it's as hot as a hot potato.

The caller turns his or her back to the circle so he or she can't see who has the potato. When the caller feels like it, he or she calls "Stop!" and the player left holding the hot potato is out.

Keep going until one player remains. That player gets to be the caller in the next round.

PLAYERS	AGES	SPACE	MATERIALS
4 or more	All	Small	A ball, beanbag, or any other small object that can be passed around

London Bridge Is Falling Down

How to Play:

Two players are chosen to form the "bridge." They hold hands and raise their arms to form an arch. The rest of the players stand in a line and go under the bridge one at a time, trying not to get caught when the song ends.

At the end of the song, the bridge falls down: the two players forming the bridge lower their arms and catch any player who is under the bridge.

The player who gets caught by the bridge takes the place of one of the bridge formers, and the game repeats.

You can repeat just the first verse, or you can include all the verses, on the right.

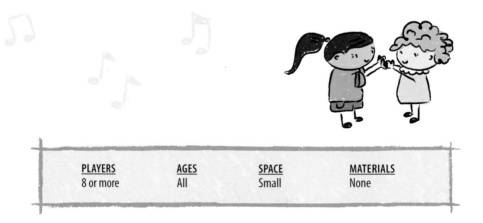

PLAYERS	AGES	SPACE	MATERIALS
8 or more	All	Small	None

"London Bridge Is Falling Down"

London Bridge is falling down,
Falling down, falling down.
London Bridge is falling down,
My fair lady.

How will we build it up,
Build it up, build it up?
How will we build it up,
My fair lady?

Build it up with gold and silver,
Gold and silver, gold and silver.
Build it up with gold and silver,
My fair lady.

Gold and silver I have none,
I have none, I have none.
Gold and silver I have none,
My fair lady.

Build it up with pins and needles,
Pins and needles, pins and needles.
Build it up with pins and needles,
My fair lady.

Pins and needles bend and break,
Bend and break, bend and break.
Pins and needles bend and break,
My fair lady.

Build it up with wood and clay,
Wood and clay, wood and clay.
Build it up with wood and clay,
My fair lady.

Wood and clay will wash away,
Wash away, wash away.
Wood and clay will wash away,
My fair lady.

Build it up with stone so strong,
Stone so strong, stone so strong.
Build it up with stone so strong,
My fair lady.

Stone so strong will last so long,
Last so long, last so long.
Stone so strong will last so long,
My fair lady.

Drip, Drip, Drop

How to Play:

Drip, Drip, Drop is similar to Duck, Duck, Goose, but with an added summer twist! One person is chosen to be "It." He or she is given a pail full of water. The rest of the players sit in a circle on the ground.

The person who is "It" walks around the outside of the circle, stopping at each person and saying "Drip" while pouring a drip of water on that person's head.

Whenever "It" decides, he or she changes to "Drop!" and pours the remaining water on the next player. That player then stands up and tries to tag "It." "It" runs around the circle and tries to sit in the vacant spot before getting tagged.

If the player does not tag "It," he or she becomes "It" in the next round. If "It" is tagged, he or she is "It" for another round.

PLAYERS	AGES	SPACE	MATERIALS
5 or more	5+	Medium	A small pail or bucket and a hose or other water source

Take Your Place

How to Play:

If you are using cones or bases, place them in a wide circle. If you are drawing circles with chalk, draw as many circles (about a foot wide) as you have players in a wide ring.

Have each player stand by a cone or on a base or circle. Then ask one player to stand alone in the center of the play area so that one space is left vacant. That person then tries to take the vacant space while the other players work together to prevent him or her from doing just that! A player next to the vacant space may rush over to take the empty place first, creating a different empty place, which another player may try to fill before the person in the middle has a chance to get to it.

Play continues until the middle player is finally able to take an empty place. Choose a new person to be in the middle and begin another round!

Adapted from the *Playworks Playbook*

PLAYERS	AGES	SPACE	MATERIALS
6 or more	8+	Medium to large	Cones, bases, or chalk to draw circles on the ground — one for each player

All Tangled Up

How to Play:

Have the players stand close together in a circle. Then have each player hold one hand with anyone in the group except the person standing next to him or her.

Repeat with players' free hands—avoiding anyone standing next to them or with whom they are already holding hands.

Now have the group try to untangle itself without letting go of anyone's hand. It takes patience and lots of cooperation!

If you have twelve or more people, split into two groups of six and see which group can get untangled faster.

Adapted from the *Playworks Playbook*

PLAYERS	AGES	SPACE	MATERIALS
6 or more	8+	Medium	None

Windows and Doors

How to Play:

Players hold hands and stand far apart in a circle, so that large spaces are formed underneath their arms. These spaces will be the "windows" and "doors."

One player is chosen as the runner. He or she weaves in and out of the doors and windows created by the other players' arms.

The other players try to catch the runner by lowering their arms and preventing him or her from passing through. When the runner is caught, he or she joins the circle and chooses a new runner.

PLAYERS	AGES	SPACE	MATERIALS
5 or more	5+	Large	None

Race
Games

Sack Race

How to Play:

All the players line up at the starting line and climb into their sacks or pillowcases.

At "Ready, set, go!" everyone takes off — hopping, waddling, and stumbling toward the finish line.

The first person to make it to the finish line without falling or losing his or her sack wins!

For variety, try setting up a sack race as a relay — the fun of trying to help teammates step in and out of the sack always makes for some great laughs.

PLAYERS	AGES	SPACE	MATERIALS
2 or more	5+	Medium to large	A potato (or coffee-bean) sack or large pillowcase for each participant; a way to designate a starting and finish line

Red Light, Green Light

How to Play:

Choose one player to be the "stoplight." The other players line up in a row about 10 paces from the stoplight, who stands with his or her back to the other players.

The stoplight yells "Green light!" and the other players move forward. At any time, the stoplight can turn around and say "Red light!" and the other players have to freeze in their tracks. Anyone whom the stoplight sees still moving is sent back to the starting line.

Players can move as fast as they want when there's a green light, but the faster they go, the harder it will be to stop in time when the stoplight says "Red light!"

The first player to tag the stoplight earns the right to be the stoplight in the next round.

If there are a lot of players, it's best to draw a finish line for them to cross instead of having them tag the stoplight, to avoid giving an unfair advantage to the players in the middle of the line.

PLAYERS	AGES	SPACE	MATERIALS
3 or more	All	Small to medium	None

Egg-and-Spoon Race

How to Play:

This game is a classic! Play with individual racers or as a relay race in teams.

First designate a starting point and a finish line. Then all the players should take an egg and a spoon and line up at the starting line. Once the players place the eggs on the spoons, the referee should say "Ready, set, go!" to start the race.

Each player tries to walk as fast as he or she can to the finish line without letting the egg fall off the spoon. Players cannot use their free hands to balance the eggs. If the egg falls off the spoon, the player has to pick it up and start the course over at the starting point. Whoever makes it to the finish line first wins the race!

This game can also be played in teams as a relay race. When a player returns to the starting line, he or she passes the egg and spoon to the next racer. The first team whose final player makes it back to the starting line wins the race.

PLAYERS	AGES	SPACE	MATERIALS
2 or more	5+	Medium	An egg and spoon for each participant; a way to designate a starting point and finish line

Obstacle Course

How to Play:

An obstacle course can work in playspaces of all shapes and in groups of all sizes. This is a great activity to do in teams, in which each person can do a different obstacle, or as individuals. You can make this a family game and challenge parents to join. Use cones, lawn chairs, cardboard boxes, or other items to set up an obstacle course in your yard or park. A stopwatch can be used to see which racer makes it through in the best time.

Be creative with the types of obstacles you set up. Think of all the activities you can encourage players to do — climb, jump, crawl, wiggle, throw. Here are two ideas for easy-to-make obstacle stations:

Ladder run: Lay a jump rope in a zigzag pattern on the ground. Have the players jump over each bend in the rope without actually touching it.

Army crawl: Set up lawn chairs and have players slither underneath them.

PLAYERS	AGES	SPACE	MATERIALS
Unlimited	8+	Large	Cones, lawn chairs, cardboard boxes, beanbags, jump rope, other found objects; stopwatch

What Time Is It, Mr. Wolf?

How to Play:

Choose one player to be Mr. Wolf. Designate a starting line and have the players line up along it. Mr. Wolf stands about 20 feet away with his or her back to the other players.

To start the game, the players call out, "What time is it, Mr. Wolf?" and Mr. Wolf replies with a time, such as "Two o'clock!" or "Five o'clock!"

The players then take that number of steps closer to Mr. Wolf. At any time, though, Mr. Wolf can instead answer with "Dinnertime!" and then turn around and chase the players back to the starting line. If Mr. Wolf tags anyone, that player is out.

The goal for the players is both to reach Mr. Wolf before he or she calls "Dinnertime!" and avoid getting tagged if he or she does call. So they can take either big steps forward, if they want to reach Mr. Wolf faster, or smaller steps if they are worried about Mr. Wolf catching them.

If a player does reach Mr. Wolf without getting caught, he or she is Mr. Wolf in the next round.

PLAYERS	AGES	SPACE	MATERIALS
3 or more	5+	Medium to large	Chalk or some other way to mark off a starting line

Mother, May I?

How to Play:

Mother, May I? is similar to Red Light, Green Light, but it allows for a lot of creativity in the way you move forward.

Choose one player to be "Mother" and have the other players line up about 10 to 15 paces away. Each player then takes a turn asking "Mother" if he or she can take a certain number of a certain kind of step forward, for instance, "Mother, may I take four baby steps?" Other types of steps could be hopping steps, twirling steps, giant steps, or rolling steps. Be creative!

Mother can then answer, "Yes, you may" or "No, you may not," depending on his or her whim. The first player to reach Mother wins! Tip: It's more fun when Mother mixes up his or her responses and doesn't play favorites.

PLAYERS	AGES	SPACE	MATERIALS
3 or more	All	Small to medium	None

Run If

How to Play:

If you are playing on a playground, use the chalk to mark off a starting line and a finish line about 20 feet apart. If you are playing in a yard or a park, you can also use two trees, a fence, or any other way to mark a starting place and a finish line. Choose one player to be the caller and have the other players line up or gather at the starting line.

The caller then says, "Run if. . ." and chooses some kind of identifier, such as "Run if you are wearing a red shirt" or "Run if you are wearing sandals." Then any players who fit that description run to the finish line. To mix things up, the caller can also call out "Hop if . . ." or "Skip if. . ." or any other kind of movement. Keep going until all the players make it to the finish line. Then turn around and play another round going the other way.

You can elect a new caller for each round. Be creative with the movements and be inclusive with the identifiers—the point is to have fun!

Adapted from the *Playworks Playbook*

PLAYERS	AGES	SPACE	MATERIALS
4 or more	5+	Large	Chalk or some other way to mark a boundary

Other Games

Shoe Golf

How to Play:

There are three ways to play shoe golf: for accuracy, distance, or fewest kicks to the hole. Choose which version you'd like to play, then have all the players unlace their shoes so that they rest loosely on their feet.

If playing for accuracy, players kick each one of their shoes toward hard-to-reach places or goals such as on top of a picnic table or directly under a park bench.

If playing for distance, players stand behind a line or area on the grass, then flip one of their shoes as far as possible. Whichever player has the longest "drive" wins.

If playing for fewest kicks to the hole, players take turns kicking their shoes toward a designated target or "hole," such as a rock or a circle drawn in chalk on the playground. The player whose shoe reaches the target with the fewest number of kicks goes first on the next hole.

PLAYERS	AGES	SPACE	MATERIALS
2 or more	5+	Medium	Players' shoes; change of socks for each player

Spinning Statues

How to Play:

Choose one player to be the spinner. The rest of the players are the statues.

The spinner takes the first player by the wrist or hand, spins him or her around in a circle a few times, and then lets go! The statue has to freeze as soon as he or she can and hold that pose. Sometimes the poses are pretty crazy!

The spinner then takes the next player and swings him or her in the same way. The statues have to hold their poses as long as they can.

The player who holds his or her pose the longest is the winner and becomes the spinner in the next round.

PLAYERS	AGES	SPACE	MATERIALS
3 or more	5+	Small	None

Hop 'n' Freeze

How to Play:

Mark off the play area, then choose one player to be the caller. The rest of the players are the hoppers. The caller starts by shouting out, "Start hopping on one foot!" and all the hoppers have to hop up and down on one foot, staying within the boundaries of the play area. If they step out of bounds, they are out. Then the caller says "Freeze!" and the hoppers have to freeze in place. If they move, they are out.

The caller then calls out another action, such as "Start walking backwards" or "Start twirling," and the hoppers have to follow along until the caller yells "Freeze!" once more. The last player to be out is the caller in the next round.

For variety, you can have each hopper try to balance a beanbag on his or her head while hopping or have the hoppers pair up and try to perform feats together.

Adapted from the *Playworks Playbook*

PLAYERS	AGES	SPACE	MATERIALS
4 or more	All	Small	Chalk or some other way to mark off the play area

Leapfrog

How to Play:

You can play leapfrog with as few as two people or as many people as you can gather together. It's a silly game that has players leaping over one another, just like frogs.

First have all the players line up, kneeling, with their heads resting on the ground and their hands covering their heads. Be sure to leave a little bit of space, but not too much, between each player.

The last person in line then gets up, puts his or her hands on the back of the person in front of him or her, and leaps over that person—just like a frog! The leaper keeps going until he or she gets to the front of the line, where he or she kneels and joins the line. The next player at the end of the line then gets up and starts leaping.

You can keep going until all the players have hopped, or you can just keep going as long as you like!

PLAYERS	AGES	SPACE	MATERIALS
2 or more	5+	Medium to large grassy field	None

Sleeping Lions

How to Play:

Choose one or two players to be the hunters, while the rest of the players are the lions.

The lions lie down with their eyes closed, as if they are sleeping. The hunters walk among the lions and try to "wake" them up by getting them to make a noise or move—but they aren't allowed to touch the lions at all, so they have to try to tell jokes or surprise them in some way.

Be creative! Any lion who moves or giggles must stand up and become one of the hunters.

PLAYERS	AGES	SPACE	MATERIALS
4 or more	5+	Medium	None

Other Games

Simon Says

How to Play:

Simon Says can be played with kids of all ages and always results in peals of laughter. Pick one person to be "Simon." Simon's job is to tell the rest of the players what they should do. Players must obey only those commands that begin with the words "Simon says." So if Simon says, "Simon says touch your nose," then players must touch their noses. But if Simon says "Jump!" (without the "Simon says"), then the players shouldn't jump.

Simon stands facing the group and gives the instructions, trying to trick the players into following commands when they shouldn't. Players who get tricked into following commands that don't start with "Simon says" are out for the round.

The last person left after all the others are out is the next Simon.

PLAYERS	AGES	SPACE	MATERIALS
3 or more	All	Small to large	None

Follow the Leader

How to Play:

Follow the Leader is a simple game with simple rules, but it can be as crazy and as exciting as you can imagine!

Choose one player to be the leader. The leader starts by doing something funny or silly or difficult to follow, such as hopping on one foot, walking backwards, or clapping in rhythm—whatever his or her imagination can come up with!

The other players have to follow along and do exactly what the leader does. If a player doesn't follow the leader exactly, then he or she is out.

Play continues until there is one follower left. That person gets to be the leader in the next round.

PLAYERS	AGES	SPACE	MATERIALS
3 or more	All	Medium	None

Dance Freeze

How to Play:

Choose one player to be the music master, while the rest of the players are dancers. When the music master starts to play some music, the dancers start dancing.

The music master can stop the music at any time and each dancer must freeze immediately and hold that position until the music master starts the music again. If a player does not freeze immediately, he or she has to do ten jumping jacks before the next round.

For variety, the music master can also teach a new dance move before each round. The dancers then have to dance that move in the next round. The music master can create something that's high energy, slow and smooth, or just plain silly!

Adapted from the *Playworks Playbook*

PLAYERS	AGES	SPACE	MATERIALS
4 or more	All	Small to medium	CD player, or MP3 player with speakers

Rhythm Detective

How to Play:

Choose one player to be the rhythm detective, who then stands far apart from the group, closes his or her eyes, and counts to one hundred. The rest of the players stand in a circle and silently choose one person to be the leader — they've got to be quick!

The leader then starts a short, easy-to-follow rhythm that the rest of the players need to imitate — with clapping, snapping, knee-slapping, etc. The leader should change the rhythm every ten seconds or so, and the rest of the group must follow along.

Once the detective has counted to one hundred, he or she enters the circle, the rhythms continue, and he or she tries to figure out who is leading. If he or she guesses right, the leader becomes the detective in the next round. If he or she guesses wrong, the leader gets to choose the next detective.

Adapted from the *Playworks Playbook*

PLAYERS	AGES	SPACE	MATERIALS
4 or more	5+	Small	None

Other Games

Giant Dominoes

How to Play:

You play giant dominoes just like regular dominoes. But first you have to make the dominoes! If you are using shoe boxes, first tape the lid to the top. Then use the black and white paint to create domino patterns. After the giant dominoes have dried, take them outside and have a game of giant domino fun!

Submitted by a Play Day participant

PLAYERS	AGES	SPACE	MATERIALS
2 or more	5+	Medium	Lots of rectangular boxes such as shoe boxes; black and white paint

Limbo

How to Play:

How low can you go? When you play limbo, you'll find out! If you are using a bamboo branch as your limbo stick, remove all the leaves so you have a smooth stick.

Two people are the stick holders and hold the stick between them while the other players take turns trying to go under the limbo stick by bending over backwards. The stick starts out at shoulder height, but then gets lower and lower each round!

The people going under the stick can't touch the ground with their hands, lean forward, or touch the limbo stick while going under it. If they do, they are out of the game. The winner is the last player left who can still make it under the limbo stick.

Submitted by a Play Day participant

PLAYERS	AGES	SPACE	MATERIALS
4 or more	All	Medium	Long bamboo branch or other long stick such as a broomstick

Other Games

Doggy, Doggy

How to Play:

One person, the "doggy," sits on a bench or the ground with his or her back to the group. An object such as a small stick is put under the bench or behind the dog. That is the bone.

While the doggy remains sitting with his or her eyes closed, counting to fifty, someone sneaks up, steals the bone, and hides it somewhere on him- or herself.

Then everyone chants:

> *Doggy, doggy, where's your bone?*
> *Somebody stole it from your home.*
> *Guess who? It might be you!*

The doggy has three chances to guess who took it. If he or she guesses right, then he or she gets to be the doggy again. If he or she guesses wrong, then the person who has the bone gets a turn as the doggy.

PLAYERS	AGES	SPACE	MATERIALS
5 or more	5+	Small	Any object that can be used as the "bone"

No-Rules Games

Pop-Up Playground

How to Play:

Create a pop-up adventure playground using loose parts, which can be any kind of found, donated, or recycled materials—whatever happens to be available. The sky's the limit when looking for materials: cardboard boxes, wood, rope, sticks and twigs, fabric, PVC pipe, paint, or markers. Collect as much stuff as you can.

Then you'll want to find a place to set up your pop-up playground. Depending on your community, you can set it up in a park, the woods, at a friend's dead-end street, your own front yard, or anywhere else you can think of. Remember, play can happen anywhere!

There are no rules to creating a pop-up playground—it's a perfect opportunity for unstructured play. Children can build a car, construct a fort, engineer a robot, or assemble a human maze. They can create their own imaginary world.

An idea pioneered by the New York Coalition for Play

PLATERS	AGES	SPACE	MATERIALS
Unlimited	5+	Large	Loose parts

Sand and Splash Zone

How to Play:

Playing with water is a lot of fun, especially to cool down in the warmer months. Fill a large plastic bin with water and add a variety of recycled plastic containers (such as milk jugs, water bottles, and yogurt containers). If you'd like, use another bin and fill it with play sand.

There are endless possibilities for activities to engage in with a sand and water station. Do a mini-science experiment to see which objects float and which sink. Think of the materials you have around the house or in nature that could be used to construct a boat. Set up a fossil dig by hiding objects in the sand. Get creative!

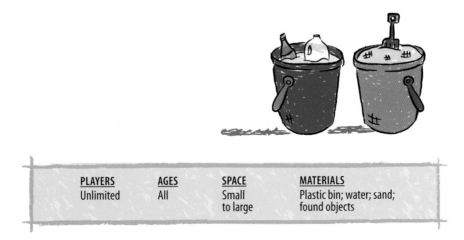

PLAYERS	AGES	SPACE	MATERIALS
Unlimited	All	Small to large	Plastic bin; water; sand; found objects

Imagination Stage

How to Play:

A big box of old clothes or costumes can turn your afternoon into a world of imagination. Gather unique old clothes from your closet that can be used for future dress-up days.

Using arts and crafts supplies, add decorations or paint old shirts to make homemade costumes. Act out a favorite book or pretend to be a doctor, scientist, or teacher!

What far-off lands can you visit in your make-believe world? If you can dream it, you can make it happen on your Imagination Stage.

The stage can be as simple as using twigs to form a square in the grass or using jump ropes to designate a spot on the playground. Invite friends to join the fun! You could even put on a show and invite grown-ups to come watch.

PLAYERS	AGES	SPACE	MATERIALS
Unlimited	All	Small to medium	Old clothes or costumes and other assorted props

Create-a-Game

How to Play:

Games don't need to be elaborate, with tons of rules or equipment, to be lots of fun! Kids can invent their own. Using three objects, an infinite number of games can be created. What could be played with socks, paper bags, and a Hula-Hoop? Or how about a cup, a bouncy ball, and a stick?

Find three objects and start playing. You don't have to make set rules, and the game can change as it's played. Simple items can turn into hours of play.

Since the game can change each time it's played, it promotes imagination and creative thinking. There are endless variations to this activity. And then you can always introduce three new objects and the game will be invented anew!

PLAYERS	AGES	SPACE	MATERIALS
Unlimited	All	Small to medium	Three assorted objects of your choice

A Call to Action

GOING OUTSIDE to play and making play a part of your daily routine are the first steps toward restoring the importance of play in kids' lives. Here are some things that you and your family can do to help create more safe and accessible playspaces in your own neighborhood. For even more ideas and links to the resources in this book, visit **kaboom.org/gooutandplay.**

★ Map Playgrounds in Your Neighborhood

Go online to the KaBOOM! Map of Play and see which playspaces in your neighborhood are already marked there. Add any missing ones. A playspace is any area where you can play — a playground, soccer field, baseball diamond, basketball court, water park, and many other spots. Take pictures of each playspace, make a list of any items each space needs, and rate it. You can even turn it into a game, with each team responsible for mapping a certain part of your community. Start mapping today: **kaboom.org/playspacefinder**, or use the free mobile app, *Playgrounds!*

★ Write to Your Newspaper

Start a public conversation in your community about how to improve the state of play by writing an op-ed or a letter to the editor of your local newspaper. This is a great way to get the word out to your community about play. Write about what problems mean the most to you — lack of recess in local schools, childhood obesity, or closed or poorly maintained playgrounds and parks. By writing a letter, you can make sure every kid has a great place to play nearby. To learn more, take the free training, "Sincerely Yours: Writing an Op-Ed or Letter to the Editor," at **kaboom.org/writeoped.**

★ Organize a Playground Watch

Creating a playground watch schedule with local parents can help the kids in your community enjoy a safe and fun play experience at the local playground. It ensures that a responsible adult is always at the playground and protects against vandalism and crime. It's a great way to connect with the community and give the children more time and opportunities to play.

★ Form an Outdoor Playgroup

Start an outdoor playgroup to provide kids with playmates and parents with the support and motivation they need to get outside rain or shine. You can organize an event at your favorite park with the KaBOOM! Map of Play. A playgroup will help guarantee that children will have other kids to play with, even in the hottest and coldest months. You could even start to collect items for a "Play Box" that could add to your days at the park. To create your own meet-up events at your playspace, visit: **kaboom.org/ playspacefinder.**

★ Become a Play Associate

Play Associates are trained adults who enable a setting in which children can direct their own play. They allow play activity to evolve naturally by maintaining a safe and secure environment and by renewing the supply of loose parts. Having a Play Associate on hand ensures that kids take full advantage of the play opportunities that loose parts present. Learn more about facilitating play at **kaboom.org/playschool.**

★ Organize a Play Day

Bring your community together at your local park, playground, or school and provide families with a range of games and activities. A Play Day is an opportunity to celebrate and advocate that play is important for all kids in your community. The games included in this book would be perfect for a Play Day in your town! For more ideas visit: **kaboom.org/playday.**

★ Spruce Up Your Playground

Organize a playground improvement project to help your playground thrive. This can involve planting flowers or trees, building new amenities like benches or picnic tables, painting murals, or cleaning up. A poorly maintained park becomes vulnerable to vandalism and crime. A sprucing-up project will encourage families to stay at the park longer and come back more often. For project instructions and blueprints, visit: **kaboom.org/sideprojects.**

★ Close a Street for Play

Petition your city to close a residential street to cars at a regularly scheduled time. Play streets are a simple way to turn residential streets into a place for communities to gather and play. You can create an instant playground, even without a jungle gym or swings. Use a number of games from this book for fun ideas to play on your street.

★ Take on the Park-a-Day Summer Challenge

Challenge your kids to find as many local playspaces as possible in the summer. Set a goal of getting to a different park each day. What similarities and differences can you discover at previously unfound playgrounds in your neighborhood? You can invite other families to join you on your quest to visit all of the playgrounds and create passports for the challenge, awarding stickers to the kids for each park you visit.

★ Build a Playground

Draw from the collective power of your community to create a new place for the kids to play. Use the KaBOOM! online Project Planner to go through every part of the playspace building process, from idea to fund-raising to maintenance. The planner gives you all the tools you need to follow the KaBOOM! done-in-a-day, community-led build model. To start your own project and receive all sorts of helpful tips, check out: **kaboom.org/projects.**

⭐ Rally Your City to Become a Playful City USA

Make your community a national role model, leading the way for play and growing the next generation of healthy and productive adults! Join other communities as part of Playful City USA. This national recognition program honors cities and towns across the nation committed to taking action for play. To learn more about Playful City USA, visit: **kaboom.org/playfulcityusa.**

⭐ Want to Do More?

We're excited to see that the cause of play is gaining momentum and attention, but we still have work to do to fully solve the play deficit. Here are some of the organizations that are also working to further the cause:

Alliance for Childhood: **www.allianceforchildhood.org**
American Association for the Child's Right to Play (IPA/USA): **www.ipausa.org**
The Association for the Study of Play (TASP): **www.tasplay.org**
Boston Schoolyard Initiative: **www.schoolyards.org**
Children & Nature Network: **www.childrenandnature.org**
Imagination Playground: **www.imaginationplayground.com**
Let's Move: **www.letsmove.gov**
The National Museum of Play: **www.museumofplay.org**
National Policy and Legal Analysis Network to Prevent Childhood Obesity: **www.nplanonline.org**
National Recreation and Park Association: **www.nrpa.org**
Playworks: **www.playworks.org**
The Reusable Resources Association: **www.reusableresources.homestead.com**
Shane's Inspiration: **www.shanesinspiration.org**
Streetplay: **www.streetplay.com**
US Play Coalition: **usplaycoalition.clemson.edu**
Wild Zones: **www.wild-zone.net**

PHOTOGRAPHY CREDITS: